AURA LIFETIME

Volume One

t thilleman

Rain Mountain Press
New York City

©2017 t thilleman
ISBN 978-0-998187-29-7
cover painting & portrait of tt: Adrian Carruthers
AC art here used with permission by the Estate of Adrian Carruthers

for more information about AC, please visit:
http://www.acme.org.uk/residencies/adriancarruthers

Library of Congress Cataloging-in-Publication Data

Names: Thilleman, Tod, author.
Title: Aura Lifetime / T. Thilleman.
Description: New York City : Rain Mountain Press, [2017] |
Series: Aura Lifetime ; volume 1
Identifiers: LCCN 2016058265 | ISBN 9780998187297 (trade paper : alk. paper)
Classification: LCC PS3570.H453 A6 2017 | DDC 811/.54--dc23
LC record available at https://lccn.loc.gov/2016058265

for RB, HW, JH, LW & DK

*Because
every
persona
has run
its course*

———

the poet's work needs be re-constructed with activations of this new biography of "watery light," the living bloodstream of an inherited body.

Aura, as j was describing it to me, lived within, hidden within my vocabulary. That is, within a vocabulary of supposed knowing, which could *not* "know" what rose out of it by way of the act of naming, however intimate it once felt.

Certainly, all preoccupations with composition were now more important than before. What would bring the newer intimations, the newer associations, out?

What would the exposing element enable toward a register and alignment of all its varied stabs-in-the-dark?

The lessening of stab, a confidence in length and duration of many types of returns, enabled through the darkness of *biography* turned, further toward bios, night, brings on radiant touch. *The entire collection of poems as stellar potency had to be sluiced through what j/j hastain calls the Waters of the West.*

Do we evolve toward ourselves or away? This question is central to choice and how choice influences what we eventually write. Through the stack of printouts, j, crossing and deleting lines, digging deep into the post-psyche of my pages, circled certain passages. All the while, literally taking in steam and a hot bath, immersed in the primal element of earthly and underground touch.

The sense of a new composition came forward. It *forwarded* because someone was more than interested in the circumstances of the poems, more than interested in the writer as stick-figure, player in an arty game.

j began explaining what was appearing from the few lines, the luminous ones, the winkled ones, those drawn out of presences, surrounding us at the moment we were reading *after* j's watery sessions.

So here was a truer register, or, a birthing of song, just as it always seemed to me from the very beginning.

j pronounced the phrase "Lifetimes in Aura", or, "Aura Lifetime."

The point was to make everything come to a head within the surrounding mood or vision. *Aura.* To discern in the indiscernible a quality of living and breathing one perceives and takes into the greater wheeling arc of changeableness.

To acknowledge changeableness as the very essence of composition. What is composed meets the elements, enacting a biology of circumstance, instead of an outworn will-based proposal.

The act, the defining characteristic of all and any meaning—the effort to put the Star back into Earth—is never merely a graph, calendar, nor the so-called dictates of an art. It matters little if that art is new or old, rich or poor, historical, contemporary, calculable or graphically reasonable.

This vast Real, inhabiting the great wheel of mortality and its attendant resurrection, emanates from love in our time—and only is it so from the duration of *love in openness*.

The merge—uniting masculine and feminine apparitions as both

appearance and the opposite of that surface radiance of the eye—
manifests in the prodding j operated within my written persona, my
"projective" self.

This takes place not in an operating theater or emergency room,
but mysterious depths and the coming into eye's embodied perspicaci-
ty, on the shoulders of shamanic, raw preteritic iteration. Or, that place
where the sun has gone down, below horizon of the "West".

In these passages, finger-plucked from the instrument of my con-
centration, over an area of time and past identity, j hears and sees and
has chosen for articulation through the Underworld, where all souls
seek universal harmony and under-standing, that place the sun has set
within. Thus, moving with a swiftness that captures essence, brings
into organization the physically scintillant poem.

Darkness at the edge of human knowing yields no "after-thought"
or pretend meta-physics, instead, *here comes the new bright tourmaline
body of cosmicized man.*

tt. June. 2016

Darting Eyes Become Their Gaze

I'VE PUT OFF SUFFERING TO FIND YOU

                              dark tracing edge scent awakened
Earth's daughter into summer
From cold blast of death
Into her only room moves

Late night and all I do
Reach your voice
                         follow out this
Tight need incomprehensible pain
Toward bliss in the prospect
Hearing you weave
Oh not but simple faith
The magic every cell my body
Breaking down false reason barrier
Out   up
                means to climb
Out of night to its bright spot
Shines a tearless wonder sent me
To soften edges of emptiness
Taught
                teaches me lengthen
And wait   :   help's on its way

I see you the end of my voice
Carry seed will burn again these
Iron bars of our life's blood
The only redemption possible
Laboring pain immense nothing
Toward one place one
          Gloire incomprehensible barely
                              feasible
Difficult release former non-tormenting time and space
Finds out who she is!   There!
Beaming such
                          light tells I'm not alone

Waiting   in him
                              tuning   time itself
Backs away from the place
And still   even then   he
                              patiently inside

Bottom my down underneath's a pool
Weeping hasn't ceased will not cease
Will all this flood as if
Ears had never been
                          clay and death till
I was born for *your* power
          waits in *your* place

Daily   unable to contain joy
                              moves me only

Lays their lock-up lives because we won't
Or haven't led
                              nor follow what leads.
If you follow to the waiting place listen
And the room's walls vibrate
For they meant to be
                              big fully fallen

O   god how I want you in me
To know little joys this place
Inside out the wonder possessed
Deep in him than he ever thought
                              or her
Must show release for then
And even
                    hands over self to heart
Whose bed created love
                                   power knows
And so we follow as we must
                         finally
Shedding former lives as much willed-within clothing

Hopeful   sounds
                    smells
                            an entire world
The only world only sight
Your place now lovingly rules
Complete completed I'm done turned
Day night and night to day
Forever one birth
                    harbored
                            sunk
Risen   burned   cooled   link by link
Chain's dissolving one horizon
Behind your woman's seasoned ear

Utterly   hopeless in the summer of her void
Love   races from the date my only birth
Toward time   my death

            Bright   note uncovered person
The station of ultimate redemption the conquering
Perpetually risen
            from daughter of the sexual door

I set my prick upon your season
Moves   animates

the world's room I sought

and found

Joy at the entrance
Living might prize possession
Heaven itself begs continue

It can't   be!
                    the kiss missed
Lips I
        lifetime would find
But at back of you
Other selves fires confined time

I want
            you   drunk with persistence
To find
            I heard   you
Never given full to the completion
Never cherished muse never possible so
Never found til
                        deep inside
Where he sits
                    waiting

Is it really me I meet?

Crying out to be
             held
No one can hold
Perfume you bath in
             soft water too   waiting

                          Interstices a lonely galaxy
Spirits rail up pure exhaust eternal
Ever glorious mystification
      name of thundrous *salvator mundi*
                              daughter's
Falling   light   too

One
        simple sacrifice all he asks
Companion waiting naked tenderness

Would meet
                          you in dream anoint
Sprites this wood
                              messenger to earth's end
Raise waves over story-book's garden
Destined for terror salty caves un
                minted
To dust the serpent's
        head deserted

                apparition
Valueless final appraisal
Full moistening silt the river's
            unleashed
Lands unblocked for ocean's might
Lengthens upbraids slavery
To wonder of your hand
Guiding dark nights final restful conclusion
Beaming our look the thought of our galactic earth-bed

Forever
            birthing longing touch
                        to know her slow faith solid four-square door

Wing's
            resounding slap
Toward him in awful regard and no flight exhumes
Unused life a
            sorrow
                        builds must break here too
Flesh bone blood   again
Where arms wait and sing
Cooling
            effect echo makes voice's eternal
Redemptive energy prime
Still the heart toward hearts

afterlife a denied gulf
Gap mind no mind reached I
Offering strong   aloft
     first
               touch forever touching
Folds spans to work them vigorously alive

Face   never round this way again
But jagged ephemeral
Even weeping's incomplete I shun
Maps
        plans
                    gates reason soothes to end
And all cycles the world's seasons
Into these blue-veined
Holds of promise in codes of flesh-tone
Father
            the all-knowing room angry seed
Shaped forgiveness in future's celestial kiss
Unknown fitful cares
                    taught the touch of
        squibbing comes
Into the furnace for compact delivery
Scornful misuse she guides while I
                wait
Watch

                night embrace
Heard we expire

Calling
                the door to your father's room
Kiss beginning   anew
Blood lover's bones in light
Paths in
                mutual pact
Together temporary masque summer
Fire we
                taught the tightened
To wander homeward skybound release
Consubstantial love twange
Align light the body's
        reach
Annihilates
        voices out of dead texts
Unmaking light in
                love you I now follow
Crossing stations and static
Pretensions an actor's
Standing in the poet's now was
                                adlibber
                        liar
Grace-summoning usurper at the heart of this world's power

Into

          womb's glorious silk we poured the form

I not to you

           I to death come

But exact

      flesh

         pleasure   pang

This realm now not its other in its own end

Out   from me

         the wedding life in life doubles

Eradicating scripts in

         orgasmic heart of unborn passed on man

Seed loose to fill and heal your wound here

Voice

      spread back reveals

Folds of flooded beauty

Poet apprehended one night

Summer's death

           records faery's field fires

Rehearses

      again play scrambling creatures

Every one tells what he wants
He seeks
                    where she'd hidden
                                        bidden by new
Arrival how he'd win entrance back
Thru long corridors many doors his sounding
She's
                captivated throned in
                                        stone
He
                    rising in
                coiled retreat from the world shone false
Thru
                    canopied dark and green hope helped
Toward
                                sky's center
Blazing bloody murmur
                                        to eat
Human space unyielding fake fate whole in time

Showed *me* her endless pleasure here now
To coax   out
                                        call her out
Hidden eternal secrecy
She too waits all this time in
Now

        undoes the naked fenced-in forever
Cradle   the string's strands
Thinks control
                        more than you
More
            than you've made here
                                    more
than they
            think you
But I'm
            tired of that
Keeping heart from principle
Furious in
            depth urge enjoys
Flesh
        guiding love would view send and mend all up
                        sufficient continuity
                                    the occupied door

Very   hard
                    but you   soft
Flushing extremities with distance
Our friendly lover unexpected

To be
        entered again delivered of another body

Now

      arched forever in orgasm

Two worlds transept

      human projecting bodies

        toward tolerance

Well my life plumbs

Effort not to waste

Fucking abandons before *and* after

Briefly

      bends this vault open to see

One return

        animate directions

Levitous

      without prejudice or

        expectant images

Divides from those who stay those who pass

TRANSFORMER

I might believe differently
In the same room we occupy.
Tulips prettify
Do not garden
Forgettable regrets
Do not droop in a death-grip
Never having lived
Out this door
What never has been seen.
My words   seek
Buffeting arrangement
Your angry mob declares
Doubly obscene.

Loving skeletons
Desire seeks transform—
time's then sight opens *its* excess?

Bios as the other side
Informing reason
Not art.

CIRCLE

What does it mean life was thrown away?
Your corner speaks? Their villages define?
Our titles deed us wake?
What does it mean
To be left with only reason?
Why the individual died?
Why we manufacture blind hope?
What are you building   spreading
Uncontrollably around?

All meaning being musters
Walks silently
Thru vibrating immense ephemera.

Might I never have access to air?
And I breathe.
Wrong   all errant   all bereft
Of the world it thought
Now finds favor in news
Machine-laden repeat
Madly adheres fable to sense
Blaring dischords thru all time.

                    I hear but little
Else the covering of lies   insidious
Laughing   cajoling   chuckling   gamey
Existences unknowing   in waves
Unknowing   each other   separate
Birth circles the horizon an ignorant species
Unfulfilled   unrealized   undying
Given dream the person
Captures   thought   provided by every other
Member.

RED FEATHER

Ignorance a disability
Makes writing into thought
Memory controls the occurrence
I know little the consequence
And worry   bite off more than I chew
And drink   sobering in that act
Without flight
Grounded   loses the world
And we have lost it
By which we make writing
Out of
            all one from this position stars
Do not want the Earth cursed
I've written mind's return
We touched limitless
Space-signal nonsense gathers
Inspiration power comes
Into dim context here
                          knowns died all
                                have lost

And the puzzle
Won a place in place
Yet unbeknownst I live
Presences ever after—
Now to know what temple stood for Ma'at's.

Herself (Alone)

My wife believes all the scare tactics
Her father and mother preached with such heat.
Virtue measured by that face's heat.
Yet faces have no heat just shallow
Not deep.
                         Our equality forsaken for semblance of equality
Evolved stories patterns in a mask
Charade made real by tiny people
Wishing strength grandeur of a mighty world.
        Every paycheck from me
Intention of a shared
Reality needs be budgeted for survival.

I've never asked to see records she does not trust me cogitate.

Have tried measure my part with faith
But throwing both our monies away on junk
Useless items plans she cannot come to herself alone
Why live here if there   evolving pattern   decision
She blames instead for me not
                         giving her the way?

Mothsdowny
mothlightMothsdrawn
breezebreathestheySoughS
lidesthemothtrainphiltreDownyfurriedmo
thsongWutheringDrinkNightsfieldp
oolingdarklightDrawsAntennaedvoicesEarthspowd
erynacreLiquefiedlightpeacefuldrawndustDrawledinwi
ngedHairHeightnoslutssweatsWetAirS
hecallsforthlowTodrownMothsdownymothlightMothsdrawn
breezebreathes theySoughSlidesthemothtrainphiltreDownyfurri
edmothsongWutheringD   fieldpoolingdarklightDra
wsAntennaedvoic   uefiedlightpeac
efuldrawndustDr   sweatsWetAirS
h e c a l   r o w n
drawstars   lInsectsr
epresentMot   zebreathes
theySoughSl   edmothsong
WutheringD.   arklightDra
wsAntennae   Earthspowd
erynacreLiquefiedlightpeac
efuldrawndustDrawledinwingedHairHe
ightnowslutssweatsWetAirS
hecallsforthlowTodrown

Priestcraft Moonlight

Finally to answer all within one grave
Hart Crane

Questions answers into the overground.

And yet his work
Unbounded living joy conceals loud
        under   her spell

Spider eyes world's concrete suck
Waits and in those hands love wore
        Blows vision anew
Desperate for my steady wake that dies
Also on platform's tiered industrial end-kiss
Architected womb-heat   prolapsed nuptial
Primitive splendor spirit's flesh duped   accepts
News no man dares rarely upright
                                        Earth   cried
You came   suspended terror reason cannot tame
To banish in hunger lust our depths in thin
                domestic rags
Til sour sound sees youth one true pleasure in-
Corporate

                as if all ration were feminine
Every woman's look
Brings me back
                        seduction must ground
Image of time-spawn slamming earth-ward

Waiting historical precedent's late arrival
First
              foremost
                          loveliest of all
Face whose sound is fizzing the perimeter
Driving heat down then the word
Glowing wood
                          sprinkled with design
Young cut moist with sap
                                      longer than metaphor spirit tramps
Resting delicate founding past
For sudden moments delights
Impermanent mind shelters
Time's ecstatic sealing true grace

Smells alone determining shape
A soul rules into words each content's goad
Loser's trailing woo thence comes to buy too high
Leaves the life-place to talk which kills us   again

                          our lyric impulse
              storied gut leaks
          action manifests loose glove
        fingering the endless fit
                          evolves weird bellies no class allows
So thus from earth to sky we pledge

                continued
                        exuberant
                                butter

Above and beyond these fragments

Wrested core to this animate ground

                walk with music
Love's eternal stealing reason seals

Connexion could hold forever bequests
Within my own
                language
May you never
                                leave

                and when I speak
            opens universal fear
Of self
                        but loves all human kind

Must   lead familial dust to dust
For wild fucking forms fields real crows can't caw
        being
                earth

          departed as we

Matching
Lust with wit
          fact with sweat
Forgotten
          the books
At the edge of desk
                    brown
          round
     frayed paper routine sweeps
Entertained by rot-got
          fearful of size
                    author
                    appeals to the founder

Creation then lifted gaze toward ecstatic choice
Sending endlessness of space

Sleep
     found dream operating subject in predictable
And flung her migh
          spatial length and temporal lode

Gibbering   ignites an unsettled heart

Beyond exteriority
Wheat-shaft's sperm and germ journey
Yet fractious deep thru companionable endurance
        rules my final place
                            neither late nor early

People to tour battle sites to intimate the ancient
Ever was and only one it's you now here

I   spun
Will not erect but thru love's door
Teaching pleasure's rising liquid's final world's beauty's enough

And circulate makes flesh words sentence structures
                extension to ear starts again the world
Linking systems to system in tone coincidence and
                        extruded matters of Nous *and* matter

Paper's sound between fingers
Bells streak
        thru tones making mouths
                    space and air hold tongues
Giving from essence future mark your own music-laden endeavor

                    demanding milk
            what land cradles redounding said's recalls

                this our sentience occluding existence
            steals creche's child animates age

Death not the end
              but in purpose ours
Spent central gravity
Hiding full sail's sex
Intelligent dream's net works
Caught elastic labial
Eternal definition

Pursuit
          after mirage spiral prolapse fixes up
Some queer queen squeezed and smoking
Spits forth wonderless presence
Objective doom flint's fast lumen's
Source all nothing would wed
Further in the interstice
              first-flight Adam
Prompts whisper from a wet pudenda
              entangled fish-foam
Bird launch to hyped ozone
Breath consumed
                        our breathless beauty

SOUNDING OUT GREEN TREATIES

he came   comes here   flies or fights here

captures his prey   his eye   eats hooded

cobra meat

stripping back to reveal blood-lined vesicle

SACRIFICE

You've heard select bird's

the primate's

diving

after him the guts venerated toward

our prince of peace

the viscera

we are offering

many years

umbilical of ritual

Into his palace
                    before long
        palace
Will remember him

—FATE IS GREATER—

Never the blood to go uncollected

                        ritualized connections
Without the unraveled   disemboweled
            calendars
        sacred shield-plates
        sacred death-doors
                pyrite eyes   embedded
                cave of exploration

Women listen
                            hand over
Mirror with special green smoke emanating
And they   survivors   look into that mirror

        the art
                    babble
                            fire's voice

34

Humming

         the center here

              forces calendrical time

    ascends
      bringing down
       pyramidal core thus
      hallowed hollow populated
do these sacrifices to the moon
Blood as a vocab
      umbilical of
                diety
 tongue-poesis
        the underworld sees souls
         thru its   averred destiny
Be sent to the dwelling where
           skullstar

      —SOURCE—

And any other we've heard
Their loved
Sacred eternal sacrifice
Birthed the voice within

These voices take on custom
Intake each desert flower

                    en-flower
              aggrandizement
You turn from wearing
              instead install
                                        collective source
                    will learn long circles
              your final place
                          interprets
In blood the sacred composes blood

Not revealed

              written *all* is sacred

Contains the uncontainable

                    releases body's pleasure

Earth is heard
        Bones again
              leaps at bones
                    future spirit double

Darkly Unconscious

Inside the mutiny urge spits

        braids hair
To break

Appearance instantaneous infatuation

        parting sharp   entranced
          slit seams
        volcanic unknowable we
          as one again will do to each and be as one

Finally
To the water

            gelatinous
        Earth
           grotesque

Arabesque

And motion
    a truer world might but will
           slide

Defined: the divine as 'mine'

Perverse Perseus arrives
    (brazenly   energetically   blobular sculpt
        stands
      the snakes in the hair
          whorls of water-braid
      grown human form

     cellular penetrations
     darkly unconscious

Each star lives the flotation
        its own possessing

           constellated

        many times
          clustering light's emittances
Sense's
       Earthly
          calculable awareness
    negates its own

Is: both hope and hopelessnesses hearth

Under wave
        over water's
And each sees what others always find
                        (the Other's reflection)

                Adamic hermaphrodite
            birthed its zeal
                from the sealed
                        hollow body's telos or time speaks

Dream interpreted
                floats
        grows memorial inside
    dreams itself a body
        who reaches universality by delicacy
                speaking to you from confines of nothing but
Bars of broken light white

                Image

Great Fires

been most thru hunger ...

But a house   there is a house
within image

precious things

containments

creation itself the rain

green stones
scattered
tongue in blood-let

Incense the revived Copal tree growing into you

Out of the blind south the un-blind blood
spurts now somehow

world-time in the shape of many

Times
in the fucking

then smoke into forest smoke into mountain smoke become ocelot & jaguar

Flaying   re-forming

          I see me too become!
                    touched by its predicate copulating

Temple of the moon

                    bringing news
                                        this hybrid this god
               and you've heard
               great fires   sacrifices

We wander
Among others

          we hear stories

And place in the heart of all

                    a magical
Shape

               tongue out of the will

                    survives this onslaught

Sounding Out Green Treaties

Toward becoming but else
> resistance-coupling heat

Where age concentrated culpable stance
Signals
> fragmentations

Density
> syntax

The spiritual sunlight re-composing suns
Realized by the sensory
> clock

Pulling
Ecstasy
Recording cavity
Sounding out green treaties
> they weep
>> toward sanctity

Squaring spatial immensity
The chemically coded universal structure
Forcing sluice of

Cellulars

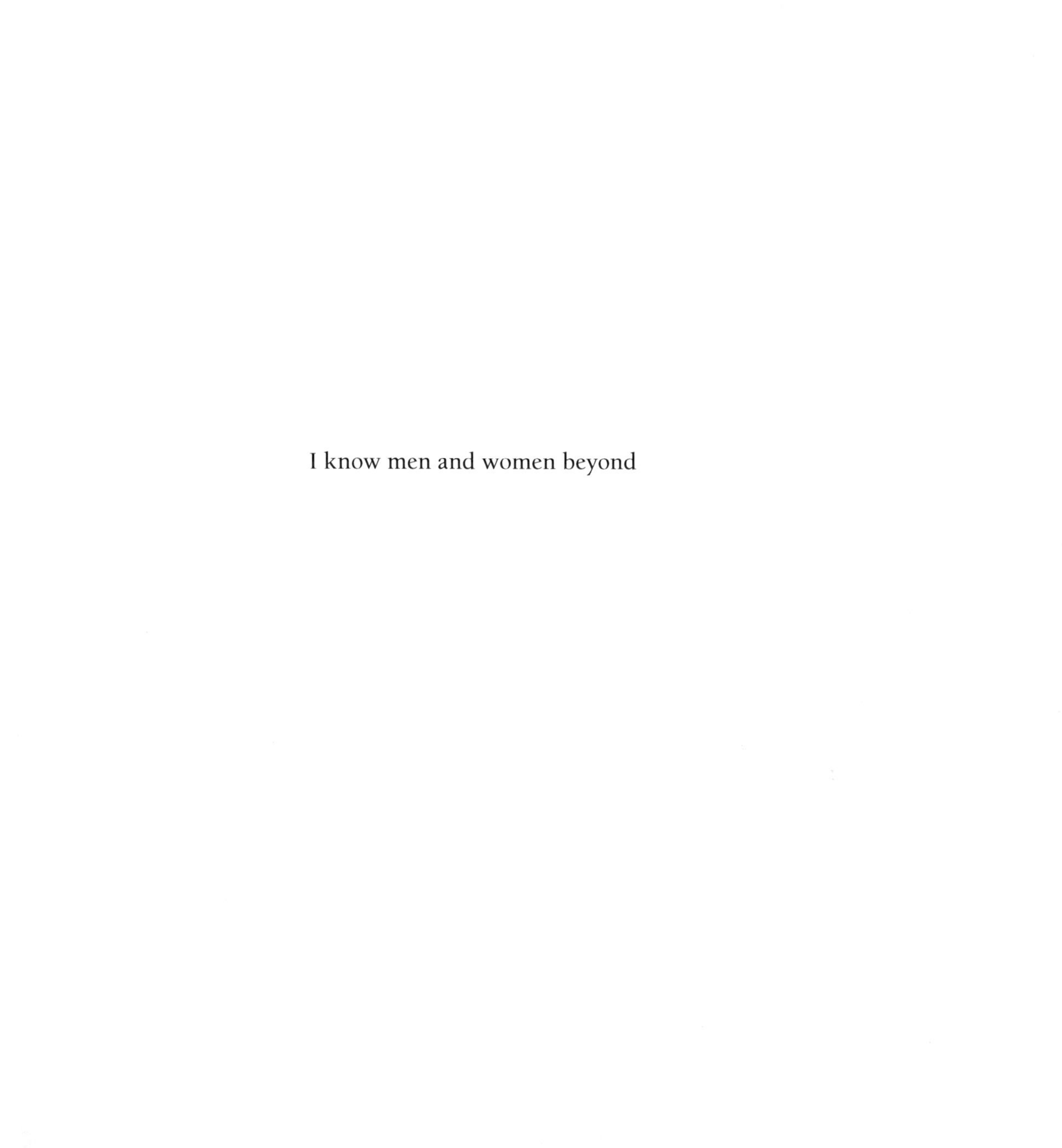

I know men and women beyond

Procreation forever
Daemon-like   wandering   fulfilled in destiny
Images lust
And break their seed
                    an aeon's light
In inverse technology   amor
Interstitial animation
              radiant waves conduct the pulse
The charter of temporary sanity

Into the rising emanation

For song in space
     these too the notes
Semblance
In bonds
Wings
           fulfilling prophetic category

Circle within the squared
                toward atmosphere of aether
In veins of my hands
Within capacities of air
These are the futures
Spelling wonder

Breath of the denizen

In the faces
Whispered sweeping
Released thru agency of sex
In recursive organs of animals

Come

All the rooms pronounced on the tongue
                the chemical
                        the earthly
Pursing for the kiss
Strong singing capacities from dark
                ability of monster ethos

Within matrix of
Within womb
Breath from the goddess
Circulating
Center
The purple wishful presence all presence now becomes

Circle the dense matter from root of primordial time

Beacons before the blast
Research divulging fiction
        chandeliers
                grids
                        towers
The spatial density
All has been given to the backside

She burns

Slipstream fund
        a penetration of the signal
                    centrifugal atomizer
We are the soul that wanders
Animal that beasts about our body

Nacreous
        carry the burden

Who

Let Composition Handle The Power

Unburdened by the name it singularly chose
Whose night belongs   sounds

    a hunk of the world's wood

Music   announcing   solitude

Surrounded memory

        its essential extension
You are the falling might of my own weight
Pangs   bloody and carnate within dream
I most admire
    with thought
How time keeps our rounded timing straight
        structures
            wake
            variety
     comply its own foreign body
    intelligences
Rattling in sound of the world
    encapsulating
Giving to birth's lineage
   level all it loved

                toward come and go
Lingers in the mouth of creation
                    dreams   craven image
     my bow's strings   over character
One mother one father

Whose traps whose will engenders the planet
                    sound-soul
Because I love you
Believe these drives closer to all knowledge
                        chemical nature
And *all* the world rejoices at our touch
                            mirrors with kisses
                        sentiment
                    coupling
                            sanctions expanding

        composition

Takes the name human animal can
                the breast of existence
The blunt night saves
Whose limbs swallowed the vault of heaven
            I am the unspoken matter of the world
Dropping down   bath of her lake
Thrust me

    take out names
      take our field of tones
       rose-bud gestures
       symphonic identificants
         womb of story

From here to the moon
System rings phrase repeated rendered
I wanted to paint your place
And sex my scars behind stones
        space projects
     my tongue shored within
I am your ambassador take me as yourself
From which veins flood
Human lot performs
Existence between event and event
Love discovers thru self gone over
    deepest waiting
  multitudinous
  artistic
     repeats
       inner vow
   its mistress speech
        routed   by
     memory
   uncontrollable environments

the weather sends
lingers
now I approach population
station of my own soul
I become the train
the halls of any abode
Would worship your tender
or any century
You have slipped into essence
the knowing way
Given by wind
Given to be itself element
edge of volcanic chimes
Places   as it was placed
hand   breath   lap
fable of a hunter hunted
My words
music-mimic pink slips
hive's walls
let the composition have power
them from this spot
interior
large world
Where consciousness should be
rounds value
laden with if it were procreative fire

Which to measure the vastness of space
Belief walked and talked like anyone   like me
Not just the sound
                in the street and meets
                            absolute mercy
Which no doubt knows to seek the deepest
                storm clouds resume
                            compared to my person
How much I swallow before I become
The mind relation to all events
                naked?
I know I know
                how profound those thoughts
All speech touches
Grasping for horny occupation
        trembling nerve-dance
                bed of hearing and logic
Unzipping maturing planes of attraction
            fascination
                        earthly fall
    Possesses the music
            presses my attention in name of it

I think I thought and still think I am
            planetary force spheres indeed

center interior said language
               image evoked this love
       position
   slut
Fascination released from all obligation
Now the heart of Being I thought my Being would exist forever
        music of a moment
    plant the single digit
   linger new epoch
      a womb its brainy purpose
        bowls
    authority's waters
   fish to breed forgetting human forces blur
How small the people seem
Within any scheme
      true powers of seed
       bosom of dream
     virginal pride white dawn
      sky of blood fixtures of hallways
    mindful machinery musters
   understand attraction of that fountain
Pumping out
      my restlessly counter-rising ego

Souls for the clarion phenomenon
            precision every scale
        ultimate value
        continuance of existence
    triumph of practice

writes   real and imagined
            blended invisible linkage
                        power acceding expedience
contentious lyrical ship   conforming
            to gathering of us in the making

This Gargantuan hybrid
    pulmonary rotations provide
        hearsay   written at the back   inside
Visions of harmony of all   into natural world
        intimations grown vital in one discipline
            of perpetual evolving

Recorded by hand   transmission
Now conscientiously wills power
Sticks his face in muddy spore
        fingered depths of deep space   takes them the clouds
        minstrel's wealth of knowledge
                    looks into dark
Eats its own understanding thru what it knows
        birds cackling on the tree above a teacher
            as time would be a topic for theory
Mother demanded the world weep
        never forgetting   a world of endless peace
                fall-out

SPORES

FOUND ALIVE   digs   glints irreverent   human nerve had risen
          self   black cracks multitudinous   changes   moment
worm's blank   spitting   segments   joining   telluric
populace
     so
coupling   sperm / ovum   spore systemic   beyond
flesh   end

HEARD HERD channel   sex   souls   whole other touches
exchange   spinning like   spinster's witness   I (beautifully
launch)   home's length   main vein versing   grooves
we blot   movement   ribbed rubbery   sustains
merge   inwardly downwardly   whole   spittle oxygen-
ates   sweet dirty   juice   secret undule   extant
fertility is utility

THIS DIRT   the mother   rounds   we   multitudinous? I'm you?
seeing   we worms   comfort   fertile   birth
world   ourself   echo   round opening
relief heaping

OFFSPRING   within

TIME'S TIME SEEN   thru dirt   bodies or was   mouth openings
foam   egg casing foam   someone   spray sperm   essence shed
stored   not seen nor heard since either magic age   might
plays work   shines again … evening   feeling
toward networked underneath   senses we   part's larger but cant
says stay   distant tunneling …   chuck them as me   past we
…   work passed …   me

AHEAD   catch head parts   orders moving parts   out the
backside?   fronting all time comes even again   many unborn
overflowing   hope by the loam   by dirt increated   leave bent?
means redemption

INTERCHANGEABLE birth   penetration   I do know?   sober
intentions?   catching on   ova   only ova.   what?
eggs …   indent   submits to dirt   cave's the cave-in
it's not   covered   astute rectification   procreative

Where Owls Go Down

situated in reality appear throughout the poem   Inter-subjectivity
of course   an alternative to scientific objectivity creating a "conceptual"
unity within modernity   (p r e s e n c e
     Technically "inter-subjectivity" and "objectivity" have been given the
same meaning
        but inter-subjectivity focuses a human factor upon the
possibility of unified perspective by an emotive Being
     Objectivity precludes some kind of agreement between machinery
denying the validity of the emotive character of man
     In fact   this foregrounding of inter-subjectivity
proposes a new world perception where understanding channels
through shifting networks similar to our highly complex nervous system
It is an understanding of homeostasis as *the* center of sanity *as well as the poem*
     The voice in the poem is   finally
        that which transmits through a machine
not *because of* a "machine"   This differs from most contemporary
American Poetry obsessed with biographical detail
     Here is a collection then molding an integration of the postmodern *into*
contemporary vision

Soft Gelid Urge

Cold water and boiling sources
      beings from a story's lonely guts
Ephemeral warmth
Idling a name
To use to fill
Lower teeth
And a tone I used to be

But we're gonna find out
    magnetized magnetizing
        grows that girl's face
      looking for rest
       my body
Right outside my window
    I want to be so inspired
I will burst into
     you're not gonna cover-up
      determines this
And these entries

Gathering one's energy
To grunt out another
       epiphora
Cacophonous spoon

Bituminous Sparks

Hid the skull   birth   Daughters   homage
Finger   alliance and allegiance
        rolls in a ball
                says to each
Sudden appearance   along rim the nature
Stellar space   infinite shape
Ritual the world over
Gathering even-tones   flowers seduction
Erects such energetic emblem
Proton grace   nor penetrating   nor blame her hair
                breath   re-cycles law
Asymmetrical generation
        searching past within present
Images will drown one another
                        stands for sight
Everything within without procreation
        shows fingers on his hand says
Material connection   all matter meeting
        contending within smoke's mimicry
                synaptic formed in awe
                purpose   cellular humming
Certain yet hidden beginnings comes
But it should excuse smoke caves
        sleep-inducing smoke-hole species under

Timing   lips sucking salaciously joyous
Hidden individuality   universal
        the caves glare at openings
                crystalline helixing
                    her symbolic sexual gore
Emblematic shaft   sliding down rough stone in a rain-storm
        total tumescent living
Embed   by me your clock   beg moist moss
        chthonic cast midriff scattering
                into the pool or pond
        multiples   pull skin
Near great mansions in martial array
        snake both to write "unnatural" love
                    a boreal wonder rouses
Sounding wave exposing her egg embodied consonance
                herself   her born twins
            even all her name carries thus
Infinite finitudes   hears the holes in archived memories
        symbolic autonomies   *living forms*

Composition to Join the World's Maw by Holistic Eternities!

                    path
            gnashing loudly
                she thinks to see by this event
                    holding pomegranate
                            moistening with vision

Animals do indeed know themselves here
                here is where there
                                is underworld
Defined by dark   the next moment's revealing
                        alien day and night-floor
                    passion
        animating   seeming to want animation
                a sure sign   echoic tablatures
                                first to echo its pregnant love
                one moment aether dreamt in another
Don't song and saga and the muse necessarily
                                instantaneously   epic poetry?
        a visage a post-time song's reproductive parsing
                            determines work's direction
Were I not the evolution the universal plain of eternity
A small moon's half-light rocks me into galactic formation
                        length   lulled
Long and big a muscular bed
                                alludes your only self

Deep Within Caves and Crevices

Nacreous   contracting   witness
Immortality my privates   reactionary pudenda
In pre and post sound
                    where his world names
Stone gathering waves   undoing so
        every single day another pattern
In a wilderness upward
                        became essential nature
                pivotal
One diction geometries channel
Pumps constellated differential tempers
                into their mantic rendering

Vibrate Contemporary penetration

Three giantesses at the well waters the root of Yggdrasil
Runes upon the World-Tree
              scanning   spanning named spans
Tolling in miniature fate
                future stature its gait's suture
Testical clouds evaporating must find speech to fill
                        fluent physical world
Apophantic bones   apocalyptic frequencies   daemon's wing-span
Where owls
              go down
                              rise from the scale
Birth true   knew and knows potential
Mating in a tree as conscious desire   hint and glint
                replacement growth every lesson
Leaping features plashing the human chorus
Crossing place to rest
                              she beneath their leaf-sound
Principle reflection the top of her concern's a crown
        travels   catalogs slope our movement
Learning into tread she comes to her dream
                inside each dream

Specter Never

                    grows from plains
Daughters symbolic world   finally spent he is
One another   ritual work regulates evolution
Otherwise composite mind shape all I ever waiting for
        hold me   for I'm fear
       anatomically
         complete collapse!
Believed the very essence of shade
Seduction of genus attached to stations
                 invigorates the true root
Used vowels in pre-biotic identities extended blood-bath
To understand existence
          let sea open ear in ceaseless continuity
The pregnant crows that swoon to beak
    breaks everything makes sense
        to become the model's body!

I will fashion a bowl and wear each look

One takes wife to find secret blue water
                    bathing beach between us

Father Lake Mother Sky

<pre>
                    scheming smart
        having deserted opposition
                worm-hole matter's warp threads
                    throw keys down
Sparkle   dear notes
            monstrous love   put under goddess opening's witness
Small depth made bloom
        marvel at breath's zenith
Husband two lips eyes crisscross
                              twig she begged me for
What stays   curves desire sought
Essence's age
                      the sidereal advance of mood
Learned by ghost binds from nerve to nude
            clothed in colors every shape travels
The man multiplied by way of a goddess
                              Other
            a feast
Cloaked couple's door she thinks and blurts says
I'd rather this were done
                    this customary meal
If I alone   really bread I crave
            benefit my friend companion
From seat to seat before the many objects
                                      true faith
</pre>

SHADOWS: TO SHOW YOU THE YEW

I knew it was possible   a little awkward but   let me show you
They   circle   black   spinning   scars
As she speaks they launch
Let me show you   searching for
But I saw you coming from the jammed corner of rock
Primal wonder whispering memories coming fast
                raised commingling secret intimates
Phantastical intelligence another altitude
Their skin and skin
                        her fist   opening prophetic time
            rising to meet two examples
This queering friendship sourced in study
        the book   the form of the book
                    mime from the rime captured
Tone attention   seam of world/underworld   finally into orbit
Spellweavers   meaning   yours   held spirit   spearpoint
Presence evolves   light   there's your verse   thru and thru
            by woman either clothed or naked
Heartache   begins make sense
                not only do see promised land of lettered script
                        seducing balances   slot's
        rhythm's already proposed   I'm concerned with finding
            life in literature   metallic glee
    scribbled a note   a breast all feed upon   a
                sweet struggle forgetting

To Move Plural Hybrids Into One

Who ever can   live up to legends
    shell this third coming I discern masks
Doors to actualize timbre
      we stepped thus to the present
Readied real emergence
        aureolic deflection tense
Light   the circle
Dark   the circle
  bodies
    embodied
      flowery musk now
        gives me view
Their need and
Our bond and burn
    drives circus of star-milk
      pixie dust
        past the passing gates

Channels and Contrails

> a sudden spelled
> determining their lineage
> bears landing circle passaging sound-gears
> Hold me
> Hold me
> splitting me wide
> Strung moans of a secret utterer
> powered
> powdered   pulverized pavement

OCEANS OF PLAIN TALK

CAVES OF ECHOIC TALK

STANDS FOR OR STANDING IN
A FIGURE OF UNWITTING COPULATION

    a wick   thru millennia
the cold vision
    whose worldliness
        until it melts
           so science

Cerebral cortex
What ELSE you hear
Do I *have* to change
Thru your ear?

        being a trance
Once lost it ceases
    I want get at meat side-effects
This energy
    when we go
Beautiful body
        night reason's mate?
There's a place inside thought searching the subjective
Spleen
Make a language!

                    a look
               a feeling
Whole life as duration
Magical transaction
               we are the words
We the judges
Is self that stays
Fold IS the brain

UNCOVER ITS OWN END

When the tiny notebook filled   coordinated poetic   wholly
from this new order   endgame atonality   any of its vocabulary
needed understand   precisely increate: the length of entry had
to conclude before end of the leaf   she comes
                    thru atmosphere
Turning everything into identity
    white veiled silence makes her presence plant in me
    all comes from
Or stays
        joyous cries from
The everchanging flood of forms
Opening cave-mouth into
In every direction
                growing divine care beyond divinity
Paper sounds against the book
Is music
Whether ambiguous
Before our time is up

*

Myself   or any   self?
    billowing violins
Multi-dimensional   (welcome)   mosaic
        some strophes get chosen and find themselves
Streaming to sea
Helped there by what
    I'm 17 years old   looking at the library
I enter
        my life   the children
Everything disappears
Those words on a page
Those poets those books
Wrap afternoon in *its* strange hour

EYE'M A

     written into   as into the world too
Goes all I witness
          everything
She holds
       what one hears I can't
Come down thru words
Coming my mouth
Death really only the total recall of imagination
Love being center of you at that moment
         belongs to the flow of dreaming reality known as time
This again a beat
Words a-light the deep black would elude me
       footsteps on wood floor
Hair deliciously tickles
Eye lights open and that *is* development
Belongs to   impressions of letters
On the writing pad sirens and
Configures you could write an endless
Thread's way
Come voices stars
The shape of heart's haloed
Language twisting
To oceans of plain talk   or   caves echoic talk
Elemental watering I'm a

BRIDGE COLLAPSE

So it is that we have evolved a language

"natural" horizon   pang   identifies   hand fanning   sword and a sword

at gate's dawn   looking for the way   I   poet   belong

The red sun and moon and all overflowing stars

Rain prolific pains

    gooey

You better

    penny whistle   bend or bends me

       closer is what I'm doing   going

Into out of places

Where you took care of me and ever will be different

Grateful   for all you give   no longer the gave   me

Without hand or mouth or shoulders thighs

Teeth and tongue or instance and color of mind

Creatureness   grafted upon me now

Remains   is how I think of   people

By luck I saw the light   frozen   antique vase of flowers

"we all share the water of for food"

    auroras

LUCE

I sit in silence of my room…
If she were here now
We would be in bed
Or better   making the bed

Are you here?
Sometimes things fall into this room
And I know her life leads the mind back
To times we talked
Touch storied eyes the radiator cover I write on
The empty picture frame
Records desk chairs tables
Including the one I built
Because she needed
It

Sitting in it now?
In mind I see her here writing in her world
Light of the two rooms the same :
Goodbye hello watery callings
In hearts yes always running   and my hand
Her soft skin body as she
Came to me I saw clothes old bodies
The upright grace in her

Poured from every surface glanced upon
Protective peace housed virtue
     of one another's submitting source
      devotes sated companions
While all bridges collapse

BELOVED AWARENESS

to embody faith in stories
statured beneath within the home
I know   larger engagement   believes   risen from matter
For there to be world there must be   unknown   must one given
recognition find recognition   of real things in a real world
Prove continuity
body finally   prophetic   vocal consonants from here to there
one conjuring ideal
folds into   membrane   just as I leaps
part of the marriage
appreciation ceremony time and space
the lyric impulse
pull a strophe
Time as preface to this letter simultaneous
fineness of line   the color
burgeoning downward growths
The pole-star shining
obsessed with drawing picture
On a piece of paper my eye turns into *the* eye
discusses pink pearl paint my nothings
inner wealth healing wounds
Love speaks kindly of me
waking in his bed how
love undoes me

Your story   from this clay
                    in imagistic crustaceous anemones
Luminescent water sparks   electrically morphic
                    psychic species
          many arrivals into one another   substances their secreted view]

Two-Fold Usage

Sentences of open air
We build more than sight
Breathing   we
Sound meant again all's place
Resurrecting nest and niche
                its nucleus stage
            changing habits
                fictions organic necessity
Whether truly known or not
                enigma born a person
        a two-backed road sense
You whose entry made all subsequent
            many times have I risen
        gulping the myth
                head at top of spine
                        experiment
            recognition's wave for all
                those stairs

Picture Perfect Living Feathers

the shape of letters   evolving ligatures curls   mirage
neither   hidden blood-beat   human goal   came to be   ground
vertical   arrived
biologies   contained in scripts   any planet
beginning an *endless* companionship   showing red consonants
stands upon   sifted dirt
psychic revelation's length   columns jointed   mansion
come to haunt and taunt   meridian-wise   hidden relative
particles
whole being out of minute parts   curling   penetrating
entrance of mirrors
beyond tells   temporal acquiescent
braves
destruction and indestructability
dependent upon her
hybridity in the momentous arc of her straight lintels

Energy   revealing itself for image

When did you come to me   unseen
          part understanding until awareness
                    I make hard
      searches along whole
                        pouring dreamspace memory
                matter patterns
Leads mystery one fastened dip into expansive sauce
            design
          being design burning stance
                  opens unconscious meat
          voices undressing

THE BIRD

Before I die one episode has to be recognized then entered and
                              taken to heart
              blending among people
                              permutations of sun and stars
                                            prāṇa *and* lifetime
We would want to parade bird's monstrous form
                      intangible body   first
        to understand furthest reaches
                              before I die

A Canopy
An Overstory

Marks   ,,,   a Landing Site

Eternal aspects   in other words   re-creation matter transiting
    semantics   language   as unifier empty   the day   longing preternaturally
(materially)   true   traversed   archetypal   vocabularies between haves
    questioning   intimation   prosaic   lost our measure

J/J HASTAIN'S SYMPATHETIC TONGUE WITHIN MY OWN

Fundamental wailing initiatives   supplants native urgencies
     storyline we have no choice but choose   galactic charm
Mothering mania might have birthed both
                              to move plural hybrids
It is a shape   determines all other chemistries
We communicate using animal light
        elemental eternal influence
Cosmic ferality in fragmented sensuality
          burning calm   a cyborg's dream itself creation
        garments eternity
                     I am spills further than your father
Fucking the astral plan awake through simplicity of yes
        names can identify if time's shared
                   constellated inter-connective penetrations
                   between two slow names   turgid urgencies
        overturning the outward inward in an isis-like dimension who or what
Isis is is is is
Crystalline psyches   pluralities of an underworld
          impersonations of liana   mandalic core
     dream come true   I can't live without you
        throat's glut   mythological gaps
             the foot's placement is a door
                   imprinting her glint with his
Gloried circle   out of the ground

One image purified the dreamer while liquefying the dream
Identification of the solar bird   invests me with penetrations
            lofty chest
      fossa trench of stars dark matter released in its many mixtures
Two make a map   close warmth
         vast ascetic resource
      ribbons their dangling skins and limbs the two of us
            fired by martial positions
         rare contrary edge   surrounded by clarity
      to settle now down to earth Shakti must accept her animal
What of the god who stays   house to house
         buttery flowers   ecliptic path
            into her book   holding all solar light
               psychic pain   thresholds of holding
         ribbons of light
            snaky images burned through heat
She has come round now and's dancing wildly for me throwing out her finger-bells
      unboundaried joy
Song beyond speech   bone-torch
            share I'd have in Amṛta
-ologies of bios and psychics in order to inhabit and be inhabited by them
      Kali road-kill   cinnamon stick of peace
               allegory of light
      story brings out all the ghosts   images passed between us
      keeping erect the most unheard chamber
               discarded proprioceptive means

Filled bhakti counting itself included
        incarnated into choice   Bala instigation
            shaft-chutes through me flying
        done by this monad   face in the face
                psychic buzz
        descended from cave-dwelling
Umbilical beloved   bends the mirrors
            not alone a machine
Nāḍi of an energetic chute
        harnessing them in stiffened sheathe
Believe I am feminine when you believe
        or how to milk   bootie the winged
        the break from scholastic pitch quickly turns to their sure melody
                    every fairy tale tells
            extending into embrace   still square
        thick sweat of all forms consciousness
                wandering in the beloved
Her merge
        dandelion or daisy
            uprising from the loom

Mergings : Devotion to Another

                become secrecy   chromosome   identity cannot
always be the only pivot for reason too needs rest   resource for vocab-
ularies   heart of every   engine   might seem   ruling   to
ourselves   portal and source
                   to stay in bowl's shape a basket of flowers
                       the skull's home
           audient spectacle
              circular association   sign
           summoning unfolding
       writing represents   writing   repossesses   poem
influence   this loss attempting vitals   telling textual tally   bloody
tongue-hole found in lost areas
          a boyish cult in heaven

A Canopy An Overstory

within one Indra
starry necklace
      working to undermine dharma
    finding a way to present
          stalls syllabic borderings
inside   knows   lets it pass   full voice
     the first
     traveled and travelers
       now forgets   centers
   now everywhere
        existence   karmic games
sweetest death-spit   compound continuity
    remains   green sap   unlocking
  Kali's song sung
        copulating contagion
        literate ligature
The necessity of intentionality   well of urgencies
         estuaries complement the body will
  udder hanging over   morning   knowing
    crossing your eyes right up in to tomorrow

Hearing

        memorization   composition   they recognize
richer   social mysteries   localized quanta   (what thought
thinks it sees)   the bio-rhythm   relates wholeness   defined
as partial   tone encompasses potential

               supernatural human nature
    drawn out both near and far

We Communicate Using Animal Light Regardless

thru all this body verdantly equatorial
testifies your personal universal
fractal giving way now to meaty orbs
testicles modulating symbolic eras
ringed upon my central finger
ribcage deep dynamic rubbing
music enters listens   rapt by desire for
pretense solely enthroned
it is a shape determines most chemistries

Each cross an erected frag   for yours
Grabbed   you by intake of me

Phylactery Ware

Sapphic slicings of unhurried hair
        deepens thigh cuttings
     cosmic ferality in fragmented sensuality
            eternal wave parting us
   faces   spoken   without ever knowing!
Unloads her body like a foot
        stepping into another dimension
   etching the other side of scratch
         acid bath   birth-stream   non-girded infiltration system
Special memorial because I bear it straight begging you hold your voice
     take up to your glottal glove
          terrestrial ease   riding   into hands a-tremble
Spiral proof slope touches touch to not
         sum each other in a focus within our coming
     reorganized incalculable transition
   burning calm my body heard
        I am
          spills
        further than your father

Drips Phallic Intention

Eclipsing all other array   human house   out of hood   resurrected erection
upon proto-bird-song sung

She/he penetrates the seat's cushion
She/he phases edges of eternity

Umbra   faint outline
Anteumbra   full outline
Penumbra   parts

not just in *my* naming
lianas
up into her uncovers by devotion
sounds her call to you
the   channel twisted

Coronal Arousal Twinned Visual Optics

containment of ourselves
anthropomorphic mines
secrets resolve in secreted   vast overlay
answers only voice beautiful face breathing essence
no one eye enduring more than ours
I love you   I simply can't live   without
two utter and sputter   three worlds
echoes   the two multiply
cosmic reincarnation
desire outstretching involuntarily
(who *doesn't* like sun?)
child-worlds
aesthetic transference and counter-stress
you   as well as *they*   I've neglected
concentrating everything now
I wanted to know you consistently
you let yourself be taken
in this world I also
gone forever   into larger migrations
cross-over interanimations
commanded by animal boar
cosmic swallow red dance chest perspective
merge binds in the victory
endures the fuse
love of contact   her black with   their red

SOLSTICE
TO
SOLSTICE

*I*N *A SENSE*   **INTERPRETATION OR EXEGESIS**

>   *Inky depths*
Diminishing predators   some causing death   both personalize the news
>   poem   held little   run-on sentence to back
Was   up to the task   I   need define   HYDROMEDUSAE
Waking from sleep image became useful
>   corresponding   brink ago   a grammar gathering
>   communal conveyance   prophecy   investment
>   appreciation of horizontal broken book un-earthed to the right
Seed-sponges   red stain   REM (ember)

          the game
     :into place the other:
       sides of the eyes
   —a skeletal form—
      skull hung in tree
           hid in family house   scorched
                telling field now knows by visage
      they knew and know images portray round the world
Thrown   would know   house would enter labyrinthine hold
        out of ashes   brothers of counting
             your passages   sits   they are talking
        smoking   stilled in the cold room's "interior"
His voice   open yard   ritual sacrifice
        bloody seed on green stone discus   //seer\\
Singing's answer: gluttony   crowning skirts and rings
       bangle   hasps   out water   clutching   pudenda
Yet here the present offers itself to ends of Earth then to be filled
        character portrays way to touch flowering as flow
            I want to tell you of my confidante
      slimey slippery seeds from the hollow gourd shape
              spreading translation of energy
       channels open circle spiraling   unending
            ministers   they give effect to my wish
    garments of our color   vest echoing some sort of repose outside our insides

collide toward depth the vortex
to make of this story   lasting tone   flood's rise from loosed now:
come apart
without channels
without tributarys
without seas
wilderness   vernal vertical upswell swiftly
half-lit penetrates the ancient fantastic

THUS DREAMS FULFILL ESSENTIAL ROLES

And every time momentous counts as ONE
      tryst   reflection's charmed
Grew out to animal relation   blob or blot
        longing roots smaller lake sounds instant legend
     shapes the water shape in water's past in place
Trance of amphibian instantaneous grammars telepathy
        wiithiin an act and further   god her natural ally controls
     founded secret devotion
    compounds of axis purity
And the heart   reflecting origination   volitionary force
      facets growing life-times

It Would Begin and End With Surrender

no longer part of an institutional

involved with matter

truly part of matter   bound

to its great wheeling the blackest black rising

Means   because there are no categories holding keys

center language to acknowledge can give birth

elemental element   original lights   to cosmicize itself

Arouse skin all handled shape

phenomenal stars to recognize preternaturally

exists in matter   arms and legs   point of view so simply a word

Infusing oracular tilt

Song or Approach to Song

The background to his co-habitation
more learnéd Durga mother
local into through universal
subject matter
violent states   a jungle of written device
The pocket   biological   climbs rearranging history
general journey alongside
No longer the trunk of one only tree

Kali's Arms Take More Than

skull in its meridian mainly she sings

Bringing breast played out umbilical

deeper than animals   true possibility hence threshold

Underworld ritualized

ritualized celebration of the lamps

cocoon thread or cry under womb

ancient clusters plowing ecliptic up down

Obverse chaff

depending on time   we need identities presented in time

eyes that see to fathom   be they no final measure tho

nature in yab-yum pleasure-rod otherwise invisible

as below so above

From Solstice to Solstice

Humans would "eat" this knowledge to initiate it
Lingam transformation skin-tags associative architectures
Long breath to teach the form
        Jasmine in all directions
By initiation
        held in wild secret   tends a garden thru the mouth
Wingéd larva   salty too   supper out intake
Streams along a border between ages
                ears   talk   caesura

Disappearance of the Mother

Disappearance of the Mother

a parade with flags floats script another dark blank screen
what is it after all?   that kind of taxonomy
so many ten suns setting boiling in pitch
emerging   milchy tits
Normalizing see-thru appearances   early   which means first
individual identity wielding motif   powerless holds a utility
"End" neither inside nor outside   council personas of those parts
what information it might have gathered   hoarded
Such controlled environment   an academic interpretation
an academic point of view
Our systemic "counts"   emblem standing for memory
plants   animals   and mind go toward one another
realization alone must rise to
The vehicle and become its devotee unending

Image Primitive

Explicitly   between legends   "within"   lands
          this enlightenment
                    issues from the base
Sight the myth   9/28/10 right now
          scape to finally walk into solution
                    behavioral statements replace their role
This book here
                    hero   idea realizes size of a finger
                         sees symbolic creation
I speak   understand   in a way or mimic notes
          totem : from sitting position initial
                    autobody itself carries signs and sounds
Encounters realities   irrealities
          wine not rote

Seize Appearance By the Twain

magics
        the finality of ours
      river's gap the pregnant pond
            perpetual beginning undoing death
         done   doing death sidereal discussion raft
      ability to do anything become a figure of time
          eternal fives   itself to every birth
Equal proportion equal footing resonance a poem hands uniquely printed
     forwarding forever to be taken personally in this wide country
        allow any sympathy cycles
                  material interpenetration of intimated futures
                subtle bodies
          range laughing into all conjoined willingness
    you mean many joys don't you?
      earth and sun embodiment two times tongue
           hemisphere north south euphemistically language
    are playful bird-song   meridian bridging distance
       reveals swiveling salacious hips
         ponders the human once again paddling
            occupied descent reenacts
     softening source   seeks the sea   uses every
         prophetic end
   discovers   the opposition in tomorrows   was out today

T THILLEMAN is the author of, most recently, *Three Shadow Inventions. Three Sea Monsters (Our History of Whose Image)* in which journal entries and poetic sequences investigate the legacy of Pound's redactions to Fenollosa's original manuscript version of *The Chinese Written Character as a Medium for Poetry*; *Onönyxa & Therseyn* (opening for an extended work, *Anatomical Sketches*, of which *Keystone Standstill* is the eighth book); *Snailhorn (fragments)*, a 360 poem cycle utilizing vedic transitions in celestial to allegorical articulation; and a novel *Gowanus Canal, Hans Knudsen*. His literary essay/memoir, *Blasted Tower*, was issued by Shakespeare & Co./Toad Suck in 2013. *The Special Body*, a second work of literary comment is available from Rain Mountain Press. tt's pastel drawings and readings are archived at conchwoman.com

Made in the USA
Monee, IL
07 July 2026

56549105R00083